The Complete Guide to Perfect Shape in just 30 Days

By: Demetrio Hernandez

According to the researchers there are about 160,000 or so times per month asking this question "How do I get a perfect body shape fast?" Unfortunately, the answers that pop up are usually unattainable that don't explain what a person needs to do in order to have a balance body as to say. Nobody tells them what is exactly to do. What is worse, they often conflict with one another, and it creates more confusion instead of positive outcome.

The truth is far simple you can lose weight with different of approaches you may have heard of like low-carb, vegetarian, ketogenic, or even fasting. It is also possible to lose weight by simply by doing nothing more than eating nutrient food in just moderate amount.

Sustainable physical transformation happens by making healthy change to your diet, monitoring your overall calories and exercising on a regular basis.

How Do You Eat to Obtain Weight Loss?

It is estimated that there are about 50 million Americans, and this does not yet include other nationalities who go on a diet each year. In USA alone they are much concerned about obesity in their country, and we can clearly see that reaching the standard goal to a balance body is really must be the utmost concern for everybody.

So, I want you to give an emphasis on the word diet in its entirety. Not only does that word have negative connotations, it also usually means you're only doing it for granted and relatively in a short period of time, often focusing on cutting calories as much as possible.

Once you stop getting those short-term results, continuing to under eat can leave you feeling awful, skipping workouts, and setting yourself up for disappointment.

You need a more strategic approach than just "eat less." And it starts with how you think. Instead of thinking of food as something to limit, think of the food you put in your body as fuel for the healthy lifestyle that you're building! For many of us the changes we need to get there are not as big as we think, but you might get great results from the following:

- Creating a plan to eat balance food packed with nutrients, like low-fat protein or whole grains.

- It is simple to prioritize protein in a meal that was otherwise going to be empty calories.

- Calories matter when the goal is to lose some weight but before you start cutting them, you start by establishing where you are at right now, and simply tracking the way you eat now.

- You need to replace your usual high-calorie intake with zero-calorie liquids and cutting back on the sugary liquid amount you drink.

How to Attain a Balance Perfect Body

I. BALANCE DIET WITH NUTRITIONAL FOOD

Losing weight may seem simple as you think eat less and move more. But we all know what happens when we start dropping calories. We immediately become hungrier. And the hungrier you are, the

more likely you are to consume more food and over-
eating may happen. Once you make poor food
choices and you fail in your effort to lose weight.

The obvious fix to hunger is, well eating. But not all
foods are created equal and choosing the wrong
ones can put the weight back on faster than you can
unwrap your next Snickers bar. Some foods do a
better job of filling up your stomach and signaling
your brain that you're full. Others, like candy, often
leave you reaching for seconds, thirds, fourths, or,
hell, just finishing off the bag. Foods with high water
content can leave you hungry because they leave
your stomach relatively quickly. Filling up on soup
and salad at lunch will likely leave you searching for
the nearest vending machine in an hour or so.
You're better off eating a lean protein (like chicken
or fish), some complex carbs (like potatoes or rice),
and a side of veggies for lunch. This kind of meal
can keep hunger at bay for a very long time, without
breaking the calorie bank. Still not sure what foods
you should be eating to keep hunger at bay? Here
are five foods that have been shown to keep you
fuller, longer.

1. Eggs

Start your day the right way with a two-egg
breakfast. A study published in the Journal of the
American College of Nutrition found that women
who included two eggs as a part of their morning
routine had greater feelings of satiety and
consumed significantly less food during lunch.
Having eaten the eggs, the women consumed far
fewer calories than normal for the next 36 hours!

2. Apple

Add some flavor to your next meal by dicing up an apple and adding it to your lunchtime salad. Adding just an apple to a meal can increase your satisfaction.

3. Chili Peppers

This one might surprise you. Not only can a little spice fire up your metabolism, but capsaicin, the compound found in hot peppers that give them their kick, can also help control your appetite. A study published in the International Journal of Obesity found that adults who added a teaspoon of red pepper to their buffet-style meals ate significantly fewer calories, chose more of the lower-fat food options, and reported less feelings of hunger, compared to those than who had a placebo.

4. Oatmeal

Okay, it's not the sexiest of foods, but a nice serving of warm oatmeal in the morning can help keep you fuller, longer. Oatmeal is higher in fiber and protein than most breakfast cereals. It contains more beta-glucan the sugar that gives oatmeal its hydration and thickness. The food is so delicious and so healthy.

5. Dark Chocolate

If you're anything like me, you crave sweets morning, noon, and night. One trick is to reach for dark chocolate instead of milk chocolate the next time a craving roll around.

Some of the researchers out of different universities found that dark chocolate promotes satiety and lowers the desire to eat something sweet for up to five hours afterward. Dark chocolate lowers your desire to consume any form of calories for longer than milk.

By now, I'm sure you've heard all the advice about smart goal-setting a hundred times. And while I agree that there's a case for making goals that are measurable, attainable, and on a timeline, there's a fundamental problem with most of our goals: They're entirely based on outcome. Consider the following Fat-Loss Program:

1: Eat More Fruits and Vegetables Every Day
If you have a few extra pounds to lose, one of the best goals you can set for yourself is to eat more fruits and vegetables throughout the day. **Fruits and vegetables** are filling, high-fiber, oh-so-good-for-you foods. They're packed with vitamins and minerals, but don't carry huge number of calories.

By increasing your fruit and vegetable intake, you're basically making less room in your stomach for anything that will not help you achieve your **fat-loss goals**. You're also doing your overall health a huge favor.

2. Strength Train Three Times A Week

I'm not telling you to go crazy and spend every open minute you have in the gym. Instead, make it a habit to lift weights three (3) days per week.

At this frequency, you'll still give your body the stimulus to lose fat, while maintaining. More muscle mass means your body will have to work harder to keep those muscles functioning and healthy, which means you'll burn more total calories!

3. Move Your Body on Off Days
On days you don't strength train, get in extra movement. This can be practically anything from hopping on your favorite cardio machine for 30 minutes, to going for a brisk walk, to doing something more fun like hiking, mountain biking, or any other **activities you enjoy.**

Mix and match but focus primarily on activities you enjoy most. If you're doing things you like, you're much more likely to move frequently, consistently.

4. Eat More Protein

It's a world of carbs out there. I'm not going to tell you they're "bad." Far from it. But if fat loss is the goal, it's a no-brainer to include a good source of **protein** with every meal and snack you consume. Your body needs protein in order to build and maintain muscle. Plus, protein is highly satiating and is essential for the health of your skin, hair, and nalls.

Try not to rely on only one type of protein. Mix it up. You can eat fish and seafood, meat and poultry, eggs, dairy, beans and legumes, nuts and seeds, and other protein-rich plant sources.

5. Put These on The Calendar

There's nothing revelatory here. These are all solid, time-proven techniques. So, what's going to make them work when other stuff hasn't? You're going to plug them into your calendar, like they're important meetings you wouldn't dream of skipping. You must closely monitor your body improvement.

For example, every Monday, Wednesday, and Friday write down "Strength Training." Set aside the time you'll do it, and have your routine picked out and available, so you know exactly where it is. No guessing allowed.

On other days, just jot down "hike" or whatever other activity you're going to do. Like the training sessions, reserve a specific time, and stick to it. Every day, write notes or otherwise somehow remind yourself to "eat fruits and veggies" and "eat protein." If you want, you can even plan out your meals beforehand. It seems like overkill if you're not accustomed to it, but it works. At the end of each day, check off what you accomplished. Then, you can look at the next day and know exactly what you need to do. These notes are a terrific way to stay on track because they provide identifiable actions to take daily.

Take this seriously for several months, and you'll create habits that will help you lose body fat and build a leaner, stronger body for years down the road. It is a matter of disciplining yourself and simply follow what is written in your daily schedule.

Many of the things I have to say about nutrition and fitness are unconventional. They fly in the face of long-standing traditions. They diverge from what most people think of as common knowledge. But much of what passes for conventional wisdom is nothing more than bro-science. There just isn't a lot of real science in support of it. My recommendations may differ from what your friends in the gym say, there's plenty of research behind my records. More importantly, they deliver serious results. Many people are shocked to see just how much they should be eating to achieve their goals, particularly when it comes to protein. The U.S. government recommends daily protein consumption of 0.36 grams per pound of body weight per day. I recommend 1.5 grams, so 300 grams for a 200-

pound person. Time and time again, I see questions and comments from people claiming this amount of protein fails to provide any benefit or could even be harmful. However, research shows that, for healthy individuals, nothing could be further from the truth.

Protein is critical for providing much-needed fuel for your workouts, as well as for repairing muscle tissue during recovery post-workout. Studies have also shown that protein can have a tremendous impact on your body composition. Because of the thermic effect of protein and the way it affects appetite, a high-protein diet can help to boost fat loss as well as to help build muscle.

Benefits of Protein-Rich Diet

Do the benefits of a protein-rich diet for a healthy body. Here are just a few comments from different groups about nutritional advice which produced successful results.

John D.

"Ever since I knew eating protein was really indispensable, because our muscle is made up of protein," says John. " Once I increased my protein intake, I noticed some changes in my physique. Remarkable visible results came faster, specifically when it came to fat and weight loss. I was building muscle and losing fat fast at the same time.

Christian M.

I am focusing on my cardio before, working out 3 days a week, but I was dismayed," says Christian. My nutrition was not improving because I skip breakfast. My carbs were really in trouble. I always knew protein was important, but I cannot relate into it because I ignored it. But when I started having my daily protein intake, I became leaner than I was, even though I have gained almost 20 pounds of muscle. I am in the same size but with totally balance different shape."

Ariel Dastas
"For me, eating that much protein was then easy because I really love eating. I started focusing on hitting my goal regularly, I noticed I was improving in terms of adding even more muscle mass and decreasing body fat at the same time. Now I had this feeling that I attain my almost perfect body concluded by Ariel."

Crisel Cruz
I really wanted to build more lean muscle while keeping my body fat low. So what I did is I keep my carb intake down, but make it sure that I increase my protein along with my calorie intake, I was the able to achieve an amazing result" as concluded by Crisel.

II. Balance Exercise

It was found out that in one of the studies made Balance Exercise is one of the best types of exercise to have improved strength and balance body. Ideally, we need to maintain exercise that would be included in a healthy workout routine.

They don't all need to be done every day, but variety helps keep the body fit and healthy, and makes exercise interesting. You can do a variety of exercises to keep the body fit and healthy and to keep your physical activity routine exciting. Many different types of exercises can improve strength, endurance, flexibility, and balance. For example, practicing yoga can improve your balance, strength, and flexibility

And having good balance is important for many activities we do every day, such as walking and going up and down the stairs. Exercises that improve balance can help prevent falls, a common problem in older adults and stroke patients. They can also benefit those who are obese since weight is not always carried or distributed evenly throughout the body. A loss of balance can happen when standing or moving suddenly.

How much exercise is needed?

First what is needed here is to have strong focus and determination. Balance exercises can be done every day or as many days as you like and as often as you like. Preferably, older adults at risk of falls should do balance training 2 or more days a week and do exercises from a program demonstrated to reduce falls. It's not known whether different combinations of type, amount, or frequency of activity can reduce falls to a greater degree. If you think you might be at risk of falling, consult to a doctor.

The following balance exercises could be of great help:

a. Try how long you can stand on one foot or try holding for 10 seconds on each side.
b. Walk heel to toe for 20 steps with a wall if you need a little extra support.
c. Walk a normal way in as straight a line as you can.
d. Find standing on one foot very challenging at first, try this to improving your balance:
e. Try to hold on to a wall or sturdy chair with both hands to support yourself.
f. If you feel comfortable now and you are steady on your feet, try balancing with no support at all to see if you can do that alone.

Example of balance exercise is YOGA

How to Get in Shape

Here are five habits that have helped me get in
shape quickly, and will help you, too:

1. Don't be bothered to push yourself from the same
stage you are.
To get the most out of your workout, the main
activity is to focus on the intensity level of your
exercise. Doing quick and focused work-out will
help you get in shape faster than slow, moderate
ones will.

2. Concentrate on full-body exercises.
Full-body exercises like squats, burpees, pushups
and triceps in your workouts will help you get fit in
less time than simply focusing on isolation muscle
exercises will.

Full-body exercises are more functional, anyway, and will help you more in real-life situations

3. Do plyometrics exercises

If you are engaged in sports in your early growing up, you'll probably remember practice being full of plyometrics: exercises like long jumps, tuck jumps, jump lunges and sprints. These exercises are great because not only will they help you get conditioned for whatever sports you enjoy in your free time, but they will help you burn fat and lose weight as well.

4. Always have a workable goals and target

Our goal is to lose weight and therefore it's much more motivating and satisfying in the long run to work toward an athletic or fitness goal of some kind.

5. Stop making excuses not to work out.

You start getting in shape once you become consistent with your workouts and commit to strengthening your body. Anyway, our goal is to attain a perfect shape in just 30 days.

The Benefits of a Balance Body and Getting in Shape

Maybe you have had a health scare or have seen a picture of yourself that shows just how big you've become. You're not alone. Thousands of men and women experience the same wake-up call every day. It's a great way to help you lose weight fast. Of course, if you've not exercised in a while, then you'll have to put in the maximum effort, even if you can't complete it. You will get better with time.

One of the main aims when wanting to learn how to get in shape fast is vanity. Anybody wants to look good, of course. If we look good, we boost our confidence, making this a powerful benefit of losing weight. Here are the other benefits.

- Arthritis is controllable
- Reduced risk of heart disease like diabetes
- Lower risk of cancer and other diseases
- Increased libido with higher energy levels
- Better sleep and rest
- Always in the good mood
- Our memory & cognitive skills will surely improve

How to Get in Shape Fast – Final Thoughts

When learning how to get in shape fast you need to remember that small changes can make a big difference. And will give a constructive and positive results. It can seem a lot to change the foods you eat and start exercising. However, it doesn't have to be hard. Simply focus on balanced meals with foods you enjoy, get enough sleep and commit to 30 minutes a day of exercise. You'll be surprised at how quickly the weight falls off, and how easy this free workout will seem after just a few weeks.

Don't Limit Your Results by Coming Up Short on Protein Intake

At the end of the day, it is all about results. And as you can see, a diet that includes 1-1.5 grams of protein per pound of body weight per day has delivered results for many people. Whether your goal is fat loss, muscle growth, or total balance body. Make sure you are taking in enough protein to make your goals a reality. The following steps will transform your body into a lean, mean, fat-burning machine:

1. **Get moving in the morning.** Start every day with 15 minutes of cardio intervals, such as brisk walking, before you even think about eating breakfast. Doing cardio on an empty stomach is scientifically proven to burn fat."

2. **Eat clean.** You can spend hours at the gym and remain overweight as to say if you don't get control of your eating. Clean eating is more about a lifestyle change and forming workable new habits. This means choosing unprocessed foods like fresh fruits and veggies, whole grains like rice, and lean proteins like fish instead of fast food or anything with a label. Fueling yourself with the right food is key for transforming your body, sustaining energy, gaining muscle, and eventually dropping fat.

3. **Have the most important meal of the day.** Most of us understand how important breakfast is because studies show people who maintain weight loss are regular breakfast eaters, but few of us make the time to eat in the morning. Make breakfast your biggest meal of the day and be sure to eat a combination of protein, fat, and healthy carbs, such as oatmeal with protein powder, milk, and sliced bananas.

4. **Refuel often.** Aim to eat three meals a day and two protein-rich snacks to keep you satiated so you are less likely to give in to your burger and fries cravings. You should be eating less calories and minimizing carbs during the day.

5. **Work out smarter, not harder.** Focus on fat loss and not weight loss. Instead of focusing on losing pounds, you change your body shape by lifting weights, eating well, and doing a minimal amount of cardio. Working out too hard doesn't help much with fat loss because you burn fat more efficiently at a lower heart rate and doing more than 30 minutes of cardio may burn muscle. To melt fat faster, aim to lift weights for about 50 minutes, four days a week. You will build muscle while burning fat, and muscle boosts your metabolism because it burns your calories effectively.